IN THE COMPANY OF LEADERS

An essential guide to the dos and don'ts of extraordinary leadership

by Campbell Macpherson

Published by Campbell Macpherson & Associates Ltd

CAMPBELL MACPHERSON & ASSOCIATES

Improving the way organisations work

www.campbellmacpherson.co.uk

Lead on!

Cam Macpherson

First published by Campbell Macpherson & Associates Ltd
60 Lombard St, London, EC3V 9EA, England

Designed and printed in England by Progression

ISBN 978-0-9573924-0-3

ABOUT THE AUTHOR

Campbell Macpherson is an author, public speaker and the leader of a consultancy that helps CEOs, HR Directors, boards and leadership teams improve the way their organisations work. Campbell Macpherson & Associates' clients range from 200-person companies to some of the largest financial services firms in the world.

He has also held senior positions across a variety of companies and industries including Strategy Director of Zurich Global Life Emerging Markets, HR Director and board member of Sesame (UK's largest financial advice network), founding Marketing Director of Virgin Wines, Head of eBusiness for the AMP Group, Senior Manager at Andersen Consulting and founder and CEO of one of Australia's first multimedia companies.

He accidentally joined the RAAF after secondary school, where he obtained a Physics degree from Melbourne University which has remained stubbornly unused, learnt how to memorise the only eye chart the Royal Australian Air Force owned and how to fly a jet (badly).

Campbell now lives in Oxfordshire, opposite a pub.

Thank you. This may only be a little book (weighing in at just over 12,000 words) but it would not have been possible without the help of some wonderful people. So, I would like to take this opportunity to say a big thank you to …

Nessi Fearnehough for pulling it all together. Marketing guru, Ian Giles, for booking the speaking gig that forced me to get off my backside and finish it. Barney Jenkins for a key piece of advice at the 11th hour. The magicians at Progression for bringing it to life so splendidly, Robert Duncan for his simply perfect illustrations. My beautiful soul-mate and magnificent wife, Jane, for indulging my desire to put pen to paper, knowing when to provide encouragement and more importantly knowing when to tell me to stop faffing. The meticulous proof-reading skills of both Stephen Petheram and my gorgeous daughter, Emily. My wonderful son, Charlie, because he'd never forgive me if I didn't mention him.

The final thanks must go to all the leaders I have worked with over the last thirty years, many of whom were the source of inspiration for several of the characters contained within; without whom the book would simply not exist.

CONTENTS

FOREWORD

This little book aims to shine a light into the nooks and crannies of a subject matter that is of vital importance to organisations the world over: leadership.

The guiding principle upon which this book is based is a simple one – we learn far more by poking fun at a serious subject than we do if we adopt a thoughtful frown and discuss the matter in multi-syllabic, academic tones.

And leadership is a *very* serious matter.

"Leadership Behaviours" was voted the #1 enabler of growth and enhanced performance in our 2012 CEO Insight Survey[1]. 61% of employees in a Towers Perrin employee survey[2] said that leadership had the greatest impact on employee behaviour. A global survey of 50,000 employees conducted by the Corporate Leadership Council[3] found that successful leadership and people management can triple shareholder returns.

And as we have all seen with wave after wave of revelations from the banking industry, a corporate culture is a direct reflection of a company's leaders.

The key to unlocking your organisation's potential for enhanced performance is aligning and engaging your people to deliver. Two fundamentals must be in place to achieve this. The first is clarity; your people need to know where they are going, why, what the future looks like and what they need to do to get there.

The second fundamental is effective leadership.

During the last three decades, it has been my privilege to witness some outstanding leaders in action and observe the leadership traits that have made them so successful. I have also observed some less than outstanding leaders and have found it fascinating that those with more than their fair share of undesirable leadership qualities tended to be the ones who took themselves so terribly seriously.

This book is my attempt to describe the leadership traits I have observed - good and bad. It outlines twenty caricatures of leaders; each one deliciously over-the-top and cringingly close-to-the-bone. It also contains some genuine advice about what makes a great leader and how to create extraordinary leadership teams. I hope you enjoy it.

---

[1] Campbell Macpherson & Associates 2012 CEO Insight Survey was subtitled "Harnessing your organisation for growth and enhanced performance". 23 CEOs and MDs from some of the world's leading organisations took part. For more information visit www.campbellmacpherson.co.uk.
[2] Towers Perin and Tom Lee (Arceill Leadership Communications Ltd). 2003.
[3] Corporate Leadership Council. "Driving Performance and Retention Through Employee Engagement". 2003.

MR IMPROBABLE

Mr Improbable (a.k.a. The Accidental Leader) has no idea how he landed the top job. Neither does his wife. From this moment on, his PA will live in a permanent state of delighted bewilderment.

One day, Mr Improbable was innocuously going about his business, performing quite well in a specialist middle management role, not offending anybody; the next moment he's running the company. It is as though he has suddenly won X-Factor without having to go through all those messy bits to do with auditions and live performances. Perhaps in the fullness of time we will discover that he was the Chairman's long lost love-child or his wife was the Chairman's favourite niece. Or perhaps he was simply the least worst internal option available at the time.

Whatever the cause of the incredulous over-promotion, a completely random and hopefully unique sequence of events had to transpire for this man to be crowned, and yet somehow they all happened; the planets of disbelief all aligned in a once-in-a-millennium cosmic event, contrary to all known laws of science, fairness and mathematical probability, against all rhyme and reason.

It is very easy to spot Mr Improbable in the very early days of his reign. He's the guy sitting behind closed doors, staring at the wall, head in hands, mumbling softly to himself over and over again, "What the hell, do I do now?" Unfortunately, instead of admitting that he's new to this leadership lark and embracing the diverse skills of his new team, he decides to bluff it out; pretending that he was always destined for higher office and that he instinctively knows what to do – in any situation and on any subject. Of course, he doesn't fool his direct reports; they know he's "drowning not waving". He doesn't fool his staff either; eavesdropping on any water-cooler conversation would prove that. He only fools himself. And over time, that is one of the few things he does superbly well.

If he's in the job for too long, Mr Improbable will start to smoke his own exhaust. He will begin to convince himself that he is all-knowing, that it was his birth right to rise to such stratospheric heights and that he is indeed a Leader of Leaders. Soon he will be giving speeches on leadership to his bemused staff, handing out "How To be an Outstanding Leader" books to those he deigns to possess talent within the organisation, and hobnobbing with other recognised leaders in his industry in a self-fulfilling spiral of misplaced affirmation that he truly is "the special one".

Mr Improbable will be quite prepared to spend entire board meetings discussing directors' bonuses rather than trivial subjects such as customers or products or customer service. To be honest, Mr Improbable doesn't really like customers very much. He also has no idea how to relate to staff, finding banal conversation with employees to be unworthy of his newfound status. Occasionally during all-staff addresses, his sub-conscious mind will take over and he will be found uttering such phrases as "the biggest costs of this business walk in and out of this building every day". He doesn't feel comfortable addressing staff. He likes his bonus though, and he absolutely adores his share options.

There's very little you can do about Mr Improbable. If you are the one that hired him, for goodness sake, Man! Admit your mistake and sack the twit. If he is your direct boss, take the money, learn what you can about how not to lead people – and move on. If you are one of his staff – just avoid him and sit it out. One day, the heavily-laden clouds will part, the sun will peek through once more, common sense will return and his new boss will send him packing – most likely with a small fortune in his back pocket.

Don't you hate that?

MR LAST MAN STANDING

Mr Last Man Standing is the more benign military equivalent of Mr Improbable. Unless there's a war on, at which point he becomes the very much more malignant equivalent of his civilian cousin.

He was middle of his class at the Academy, scraped through pilot's course, became an average transport aircraft pilot and watched his more ambitious, talented and energetic course mates leave to become airline pilots, merchant bankers and captains of industry. Twenty five years on, he's an Air Commodore in charge of thousands of people, billions of pounds worth of equipment and responsible for providing air cover to ground troops in a far off land. And you thought Mr Improbable was dangerous!

If we are lucky, Mr Last Man Standing will take his OBE (or his Knighthood if it was a really big war) and move directly into retirement once his commission has run its course. He is destined to become Captain of his local golf club, commanding the committee with a fist of iron and forever regaling the members of his exploits in the service of Her Majesty. Some of the Army or SAS variants of the species decide to join the world of business instead. The good ones become Mission Men.

MR RABBIT-CAUGHT-IN-THE-HEADLIGHTS

Some leaders never quite seem to be able to move on beyond the "Oh my God, what do I do now?" phase. They interviewed exceptionally well, their CVs were impressive, their references were impeccable, but as they say in the fine print of many an investment product, "past performance is no guarantee of future success".

For some inexplicable reason, from the very moment that Mr Rabbit-Caught-in the-Headlights is appointed to the new role, he becomes overwhelmed and impotent.

No amount of coaching or cajoling can rouse him from the incompetency coma that has befallen him. He knows what he should be doing, but he just can't bring himself to do it. He sees the 'what' as clear as day, he grasps the wisdom of the 'why', but he draws a complete blank when it comes to the 'how'. You have got to feel sorry for him really. The best, if not the only, decision Mr Rabbit-Caught-in the-Headlights could now make is to allow someone to take him by the hand, lead him down to the nearest travel agent, send him on a nice warm holiday and let him have his old job back when he returns. The worst thing he could do is to look at his new business card and convince himself he can do the job. That way lays Mr Improbable. Don't go there.

MR EXCITABLE

Mr Excitable is the perennial optimist. His glass isn't half full, it is overflowing. Everything is an opportunity. He can see new markets, new customers, and new products that have previously gone entirely unnoticed by entire swathes of the population.

He can invest millions without blinking, justified simply by his strength of conviction. He can see the sort of "big picture" that is beyond the vision of his minions, and his passion and conviction are infectious and, dare I say, exciting.

He is passionate about the future, passionate with customers, passionate with shareholders, and passionate with staff. He has new ideas on the hour, every hour. He bypasses his direct reports because there is simply too much to be done to waste time on such antiquated protocols. He is forever perfecting marketing material and presentations. He is never satisfied and yet always "up". He sends daily emails whilst on holiday. He BBMs from the train. He tweets from the taxi. He LinksIn at midnight. He Facebooks on the weekends.

Mr Excitable is exhausting.

It may come as no surprise to know that Mr Excitable is strategic by nature. He has borrowed from the lexicons of McKinseys, Bain & Co and the Boston Consulting Group. He lives most of his life "at 10,000 feet" but will "drill down" into key issues when they come to his attention. "From the get-go" he will be "going forward" and "touching base offline" with frightening frequency. He has several people "on his radar". He will call at strange hours just to give you a "heads up" and expects "110%" from his people. He is forever "brainstorming" ideas and "workshopping" solutions He turns nouns into verbs with alarming regularity.

Mr Excitable is also a sales, marketing, advertising and customer service guru. If you happen to be one of the poor sods whose business card hints that you should actually be responsible for one of these areas, you have my condolences. Mr Excitable will never leave you alone. You won't get the chance to learn by your mistakes as you won't get the chance to make any. The incredibly frustrating thing is that Mr Excitable is very rarely wrong when it comes to matters of brand, advertising and customer contact. He does know; he wasn't kidding. Somehow this only serves to make it worse. But hold on tight and enjoy the ride. You may just learn something.

If you happen to be in the fortunate position to be in charge of a back-stage department like finance, IT, compliance, operations or HR, you are safe; Mr Excitable finds these mind-achingly dull. As long as you deliver the outcomes he requires, you can just get on with it. Until something goes wrong that is, and then you're all his. If you survive the oncoming onslaught, he will never quite trust your judgement completely ever again. Sorry.

What to do with the effervescent Mr Excitable? If you are on the board, realise that this man could turn out to be one of your most valuable assets. He has the potential to deliver outstanding results and eye-watering growth. Your challenge is to maintain his inexhaustible energy and his glass-always-completely-full approach to the business but channel it to be more consistent and sustainable. You need to place a very strong and confident numbers man or compliance guru alongside Mr Excitable. However, this steadying counter-weight must be someone he respects who will direct his enthusiasm and temper his tendency to spend first and ask questions later.

Every new business start-up venture needs a Mr Excitable; accompanied by an angel investor with very deep pockets.

MR INTIMIDATOR

Walk through the imposing doorway of any number of Gentlemen's club off Pall Mall and you will come face to jowl with harrumphing packs of Mr Intimidators. What is the collective noun for voluminous, booming, blustering, arrogant Captains of Industry? A bulldozer? A foghorn? A liquidation perhaps?

Mr Intimidator runs the listed company of which he is CEO or Chairman (or, to the continual consternation of the shareholders – both) as if it was his own. He started the company, or inherited it, and just because he was gracious enough to allow pension funds and investment houses to fund his audacious expansion programs, that does not give them the right to exert a gnat's appendage of control over his baby. He is the one who has made them all rich. It matters not that these parasitic interferers may now own the majority of the firm; they can just sit quietly and collect their dividends – or go and invest somewhere else.

Mr Intimidator is completely unburdened by self-doubt. Shareholders loathe him in spite of, and sometimes through some twisted tall poppy syndrome even because of, the returns he delivers for them, but mainly due to the fact that he treats them with utter contempt. As an employee, if you

AAAGH...

are one of his chosen few, you will enjoy riches beyond your wildest and wettest dreams. If you're not in the inner circle, you will be looking for alternative employment quicker than you can say "unfair dismissal". Although, one thing you can say about Mr Intimidator is that he pays people extremely well on their way out. It saves an extraordinary amount of time and aggravation. It's just good business.

Mr Intimidator cannot help but surround himself with Yes Men. For these Executive-level head-nodders, it's not such a difficult choice to make – either swallow your individuality, ignore your principles, agree with the boss about everything and pocket your million a year; or rummage through the attic to locate your lost scruples, dust them off and join the ranks of the jobless.

However, the Non-Executive head-nodders on the board will realise they aren't being paid enough to cope with the fallout once things go pear-shaped. Because it is inevitable that Mr Intimidator's day will come. No-one can trample over colleagues and dismiss shareholders forever. One year, the ever-expanding number of ignored corporate elephants will be found to have taken residence in an ever-increasing number of rooms and will have reached critical mass. All of these pesky pachyderms (to brazenly mix my metaphors) will come home to roost and Mr Intimidator's time will be up. Tens of millions of pounds, several wives, countless mistresses, a cellar full of Margaux's finest and enough gourmet cuisine to feed a full-strength regiment for many a year will all have flowed through his corporate Amex, but at some point in time it will all come crashing down around him.

One day he will be a Master of the Universe, the next he will be stripped of his Bentley and forced to hail a cab for himself.

But put away your handkerchief. There is no need to worry unduly. He's having a spot of lunch with Sir Fortitude-Smythe next week and before you know it, he'll be popping up on the boards of any number of FTSE 100 companies. And the following week he's meeting with the City's finest venture capital firms to plan a raid on his old business to take it private again.

If they think they've written off Mr Intimidator, they can damn well think again. Like the proverbial bad penny, Arnold Schwarzenegger, Clintons various, Noel Edmunds, and Tony Blair - he'll be back.

MISS BOTOX

With a chemically-induced look of permanent surprise, Miss Botox is eternally paranoid … and one could argue that she has every right to be. She is a lettuce-leaf thin, gym-addicted, Salade Nicoise and white wine spritzer, thirty-something single woman in a world of overweight, golf-obsessed, filet mignon and Chateauneuf, middle-aged married men.

She is most likely in the wrong industry. She is almost certainly in the wrong job. Either way, she needs help.

Miss Botox was promoted to her Peter Plateau[4] quite early in her career and has stayed with the company well beyond her sell-by date, always believing that the promotion for which she is long overdue is just around the corner.

Unfortunately, Miss Botox seems to have taken the superset of the least desirable traits of all of the worst managers she has ever worked for and incorporated them into her own personal management style. She takes the best ideas from her staff and passes them off as her own. She pits her team members against each other in some misconstrued version of the benefits of friendly competition. She blatantly plays favourites, and changes her favourites daily.

---

[4] *The Peter Principle*. Dr. Laurence J. Peter; Raymond Hull (1970). The central premise of the book is that all managers are eventually promoted to their level of incompetence to stay there for the remainder of their careers, thus reaching their "Peter Plateau".

Miss Botox looks at life and career as a race; a competition that produces clearly-defined winners and clearly-defined losers. But it is not a race she is winning. She sees challengers and competitors everywhere. She experiences genuine physical pain when her peers are promoted. She works to keep her subordinates below her in the pecking order at every opportunity. She mistrusts women who are more junior, especially if she believes them to be: a) cleverer than she is, b) more attractive, or heaven forbid c) both.

She believes in using all of her assets (and yet she doesn't actually realise what they are) and has decided that flirting outrageously with senior male executives is one of the best ways to get ahead. She treats the post-room boys with utter disdain.

Miss Botox finds men her own age to be puerile and pointless; immeasurably preferring the sophistication and, let's not be afraid to admit it, the earning capacity, of older men. Naturally, she's dating one of the Board members. He has two houses, a Mediterranean villa, a yacht, an off-shore bank account, a corporate expense account, a wife and three kids. He promises he will leave his wife soon; he's just waiting for the right moment. The delay has something to do with his wife's inheritance.

Deep down, Miss Botox is a competent, perhaps even talented, individual capable of delivering brilliant results through her people. She's just insecure; a fact she prefers to believe has been kept hidden from the rest of the organisation. In her mind, she is an up-and-coming Wonder Woman. All she needs is the right husband, the two perfect kids – and of course, the seat on the board. However, she has convinced herself that her best route to success is to emulate Ms Ironballs; to be bigger and tougher than all the men around her. She's wrong of course, but she needs help to realise that there are better ways to fulfil her ambitions.

Miss Botox needs to be jolted out of her downward spiral. Her entire operating system requires rebooting. She needs a mentor who can help her to appreciate her strengths and understand her weaknesses. She needs a coach who can reset her expectations. She needs to learn how a good manager should behave to get the most out of their team and what a great leader looks like. She needs someone to invest in her development and put her on the path to genuine success.

If that doesn't happen, Miss Botox needs to hand in her resignation, sell her apartment, buy a one-way ticket to Goa and find herself. But without guidance, she may be looking a rather long time.

THE MINI-ME

You don't have to be a self-confessed evil madman hell-bent on global domination from your underground lair to know how to manufacture one of these little critters. Mini-Mees of all persuasions can be found scampering through the corridors of power as they follow their mentors' every footsteps, copying their every actions.

Little clones of Mr Batten-Down-the-Hatches can be seen scurrying around many a Finance Department, red pens at the ready. The Sales Department's scrum of trainee Mr One-of-the-Boys can be heard from miles away regaling one another with exaggerated tales of conquest. And Mr Growthman will have his duplicate out in the far flung regions of the galaxy evangelising about the boundless opportunities ahead.

Like flared trousers, plutonium, politicians and Caribbean bananas, the vast majority of Mini-Mees have a shelf-life. Maybe it has something to do with the cloning process, but their life expectancy is much shorter than other species of leader. They will either be culled by Head Office, discarded by their Creator, or promoted to their boss's recently vacated role – all for the simple reason that no organisation can truly afford to hire two people to do the same job.

MR VELCRO HANDS

No good idea escapes Mr Velcro Hands. No matter from where they originated; no matter who came up with them; good ideas stick to Mr Velcro Hands like glue.

Mr Velcro Hands pops up in every promising new project or new account win. A new staff member proposes an innovative idea; Mr Velcro Hands proposed it years ago, and yes, the time is now right for him to lead the implementation. The new ad scoops the advertising awards; and sure enough, it's good old Mr Velcro Hands' name on the credits.

Of course, his staff members are the ones we should envy. Benefiting from the astute patronage of Mr Velcro Hands, their good ideas are now finally able see the light of day. It matters not that his staff may not appear to receive the full credit that they feel they deserve. They can bask in the reflected glow of Mr Velcro Hands' fame; and surely that is enough reward for anyone.

What to do with Mr Velcro Hands? Mentoring is useless as any good ideas will swiftly be broadcast under new authorship. Why not send him a copy of this book with this page earmarked and the word "STOP!" written in big red letters above the illustration. It is not very subtle, but it might just work.

MR TEFLON

Mr Teflon is the ying to Mr Velcro Hands' yang. He is the proton to Mr Velcro Hands' electron. He is Clark Kent, dark matter, the mirror image; he is the polar opposite of Mr Velcro Hands. Nothing sticks to Mr Teflon.

Mr Teflon is the consummate politician. And so he should be, for that is pretty much all he has been doing for the last twenty years. He sees business through a completely different lens than most mortals. Business has nothing to do with customers or products or service or marketing or even numbers; it is simply about making sure you look better than the person next to you.

Mr Teflon is a master at playing the probabilities. It is a well-known fact that eight out of ten projects don't produce the results they set out to deliver, so with an unassailable logic, Mr Teflon does his utmost to disassociate himself from all of them. He escapes the fallout from the first eight and then elegantly damns with faint praise the lucky fools responsible for the two that were successful. He knows that according to the immutable laws of probability, they are bound to come a cropper next time. Mr Teflon plays the long game. He knows the odds will work in his favour over time.

In a style of which Mr Last Man Standing would be proud, Mr Teflon is also a master at re-writing history. Taking full advantage of the fact that he has been in the company far longer than every single one of his peers, Mr Teflon loves to tell stories in which he is cast as the hero alongside several of the well-known legendary characters from the company's glory days.

Mr Teflon has transformed patronising into an art form. Every compliment arrives with its own carefully honed double edge. Every criticism is tinged with a heart-felt sense of pity that publicly parades his "caring side" for all to see. Mr Teflon also has a contingency plan for every situation. The numbers may not have come in as planned but don't worry, he's disciplined the person responsible and has a detailed presentation on how the team will make up the shortfall next year. The task wasn't completed in time for the meeting, so he apologises profusely on behalf of the person to whom he delegated the task and recommends that the guilty party be marked down in their talent assessment later in the year. Mr Teflon avoids responsibility like a super model avoids food; with a delicate but deliberate side step that is almost imperceptible to the untrained eye.

A significant number of people have asked me what to do with a Mr Teflon. Is he saveable? Is he salvageable? Back in the 1980s, when Japanese companies ruled the world, their versions of Mr Teflon would be granted a grandiose yet meaningless title, a large mahogany desk, a new stapler, a large bottle of whisky and told to sit in the corner.

Employing a mentor may seem like a good idea at first but many an executive coach has attempted to convert Mr Teflon into an accountability-accepting, fully functioning member of the leadership team - only to be met with a pitying look and a shake of the head as the mentor has had to be educated as to how things really work in the world of business. Booking him on the next Leadership Development Programme is bound to backfire as Mr Teflon will cast scorn on the instructor and the course work at every opportunity.

My advice is to give him a grandiose yet meaningless title, a large mahogany desk, a new stapler, a large bottle of whisky and tell him to sit in the corner. But who's to criticise? Mr Teflon is relaxed, well off and set to retire on a pension plan that most elected politicians would kill for.

MS IRONBALLS

Ms Ironballs is a caricature of a caricature. She's so obvious, she shouldn't exist. In fact, many people believe that this species of leader died off in the eighties after Demi Moore's one-dimensional portrayal of the shoulder-padded, power-suited sexual predator in *Disclosure*.

But it was not to be. Like the last few remaining dinosaurs somehow left alive after a gigantic meteor had obliterated their kin, you can still see a few variants of Ms Ironballs charging frantically, but aimlessly, about the world of business.

Some varieties of the species are content with out-drinking and out-swearing every man in the company. They can jump start tractors and have been known to eat entire sheep for breakfast. The rumours that they are prone to wearing sensible shoes and drive tanks for the Territorial Army on the weekend are of course unfounded and completely scurrilous. Some variations of the Genus Ferrum Testiculus are hell-bent on rising to the very top of the organisation by being much badder and far meaner than any male would dare to be.

GRRR...

However, there are some traits that every single version of Ms Ironballs shares – the belief that the only way to get on is to work harder than anyone else, be smarter than anyone else, never make a mistake, show no mercy and step on as many people as possible on your way to the top.

To say she is driven would be the understatement of the millennium and a Blinding Glimpse of the Obvious. Her determination to win is Genghis Khan-esque in its intensity and to quote her Mongolian alter-ego, "All who surrender will be spared; whoever does not surrender but opposed with struggle and dissension, shall be annihilated." Gore Vidal's oft-quoted words are equally apt, "It is not sufficient that I succeed, all others must fail."

Ms Ironballs needs no convincing that management concepts such as quality circles, communities of interest and even "teams" are lily-livered and leave too much room for error. The only way to get things done is through command and control, and she's the one in control. In fact, Ms Ironballs is not even a good team player when she's Captain, modelling herself more on Captain Queeg[5] than Captain Stubing[6].

However, Ms Ironballs can be turned. In fact you need her. Her talents for brutal prioritisation and delivering results come-hell-or-high-water will be lacking in most areas of your business and need to be harnessed. The only way to change her behaviour will be to make *how* she delivers just as important to her as *what* she delivers. That will require linking an outrageous share of her bonus directly to her behaviours, and making it crystal clear that unless she changes the way she leads, manages and operates, she has gone as far as she is ever likely to go; promotion is off the table.

Of course, this is easy for me to say from the safety of my laptop. You may need a Kevlar vest, a chair, a whip and a stiff scotch before you go into the ring, but as you enter the Big Top and your trusted assistant gently opens the cage door, just remember that deep down inside, even the fiercest, most protective and vicious lion is really just a soft little pussy cat wanting to have his tummy tickled every now and then.

Underneath that velociraptor exterior lies a talented leader that when channelled appropriately can achieve extraordinary things and be a joy to work for. Honest.

---

[5] Played by Humphrey Bogart in *The Caine Mutiny* 1954. The ruthless Captain Queeg finally collapses under pressure.
[6] Captain of *The Love Boat*, 1977. Kind, even-tempered, bald fella.

MRS I-LOVE-WORK-IT-GETS-ME-AWAY-FROM-THE-KIDS

Imagine a world devoid of office politics, where people focus on delivering what needs to be done, where leaders lead by example and clarity reigns. Welcome to the world of Mrs I-Love-Work-It-Gets-Me-Away-From-The-Kids.

She doesn't have time to mess around with office politics so she simply doesn't play. She's not here for a career; she's here for the coffee – and the chance to feel like a valued member of society once again. After several mind-numbing years where Postman Pat was the most stimulating read of the day, she awoke one day to realise that she had begun to find deeper meaning in the Teletubbies and had started shouting at Wendy to stand up for herself and stop letting Bob The Builder get away with being so completely useless at his job. As much as she loved her gorgeous, grubby, angelic little offspring, she had to either re-join the workforce or lose her mind.

Mrs I-Love-Work-It-Gets-Me-Away-From-The-Kids doesn't faff around like her male colleagues. She is in the office at nine sharp and has to leave on the stroke of five to relieve

the Nanny. She achieves more in three days than her male counterparts do in five. She never works from home; not at evenings or weekends or even during the two days she "has off" (if you can call feeding, changing, patching up, entertaining and running around after two toddlers from dawn to dusk "time off").

While it may have been born out of necessity, her uber-efficiency is quite something to behold. She doesn't need to work after hours. Her meetings are properly organised with meaningful agendas and clear actions. Her emails are short and to the point. She rarely goes to lunch, but does step out for the odd spot of shopping; her reward to herself for looking after the kids for all those years. Her people have clear objectives and know exactly what they need to do to achieve them, by when and how they are to behave whilst they do. She spends time on their development because they are the legacy she will leave behind. Her work will be forgotten, as everyone's is eventually, but the people she has nurtured will live on and achieve great things.

After a while, she will "do the math" as they are prone to saying on the other side of the Atlantic, and will come to realise that after tax, childcare, shopping, lunches and work clothes, she is left with enough cash for a family dinner at Pizza Express and a one week camping holiday in the New Forest. At some point she will, with mixed feelings, give up her job. Her staff will stay in touch, because she is the best manager they have had. She may well be the best they ever have.

The vast majority of companies completely ignore this buried treasure they have within their midst. And yet Mrs I-Love-Work-It-Gets-Me-Away-From-The-Kids is a living, breathing, exemplary model of how to manage people effectively and how to lead a team to deliver. If all of your senior people could work like Mrs I-Love-Work-It-Gets-Me-Away-From-The-Kids your business would achieve great things. Your people would be happy and motivated, your customers would be advocates of your business and your shareholders would be delighted with their returns.

The best thing to do with this under-utilised asset is to use her as a mentor for other managers; use her as an example for other leaders to emulate. However, you might just have to sort out some extra child-care – and some Pizza Express vouchers wouldn't go amiss.

MR SEVEN HABITS

Mr Seven Habits has purchased every fashionable business book the moment it was published. Worse than that, he has read all of them. Even worse still, he has memorised every single word and bombards his staff with pertinent pearls of wisdom at every opportunity.

One week he's *Eating the Big Fish*[7], the next he's trying to discover *Who Moved (His) Cheese*[8], a week later he's got his people being *One Minute Managers*[9], and *Awakening the Giant Within*[10]. By the end of the month his team are busy transforming their customers into *Raving Fans*[11]. He's even done some funny thing with penguins and icebergs. Every part of his department is littered with *Fish!*[12] bulletin-boards, and slogans scream out from every wall: *"Choose Your Attitude!", "There's no "I" in TEAM!", "Strategy without delivery is a dream, delivery without strategy is a nightmare!"*. The man is a walking Hallmark card.

Mr Seven Habits has a framed, signed photo of Stephen Covey[13] sitting in pride of place atop the obscenely large

[7] *'Eating the Big Fish'* by Adam Morgan. John Wiley & Sons 1999
[8] *'Who Moved my Cheese?'* by Spencer Johnson. Vermilion 1999
[9] *'The One Minute Manager'* by Kenneth Blanchard & Spencer Johnson. Fontana 1990
[10] *'Awaken the Giant Within'* by Anthony Robbins. Pocket Books 2001
[11] *'Raving Fans!'* by Kenneth Blanchard & Sheldon Bowles. Jossey Bass. 1996
[12] *'Fish!'* by too many authors to mention, with a foreword by Ken Blanchard obviously! Hodder Paperbacks 2002
[13] Author of *'The Seven Habits of Highly Effective People'*. Simon & Schuster. 2004
[14] *'The Innovator's Dilemma'* by Clayton M. Christensen. Harvard Business School Press. 1997
[15] *'In Search of Excellence'* by Robert H Waterman Jr & Tom Peters. Profile Books 2004

book shelf in his office. He has read every one of Anthony Robbins' books and waits impatiently for the next one.

However, when confronted with a real-life business issue or management problem, his only response is to quote from *The Innovator's Dilemma*[14] or *In Search of Excellence*[15]. He may as well carry a large bag full of fortune cookies to meetings and plunge his hand in to retrieve one whenever a decision needs to be made. His meetings go on for interminable periods of time without ever reaching a conclusion, except to set the date for the next one, of course.

The books he badly needs to read are *How to Make A Decision, How to Take Responsibility and Actually Achieve Something, How to Relate to Humans, Why People Don't Like Being Preached At* and *How to Lead People in the Real World*. Unfortunately, Ken Blanchard hasn't written them yet, but as soon as he does the signed first editions will instantaneously find themselves in a position of prominence on the bookshelf behind Mr Seven Habits' faux mahogany desk. However, these fine tomes will be destined to gather dust, as these are the only books that Mr Seven Habits won't ever get around to reading.

To Mr Seven Habits, leadership consists of adopting the stance of a Statesman and dispensing wisdom from a position of authority. He equates business success with speech-making rather than execution. Mr Seven Habits is certainly not a verb. He has a great deal in common with Mr Superficial but lacks the self-awareness to recognise the likeness. Unfortunately for him, he lacks the durability of Mr Teflon. If he doesn't change, Mr Seven Habits is destined to be shown the door and forever lament the organisation's inability to understand what he was saying or implement his incredible ideas.

To prevent this almost inevitable final chapter, Mr Seven Habits needs to be enrolled in a leadership development programme – not as an instructor, but as a participant. At least you know he understands the importance of personal development. He now needs to understand that reading is not enough; that other forms of development are required to become the sort of leader he wishes to be. If you can help him understand that to become an extraordinary leader, he will need to do more than just talk about it, you will have done him, the company and his long suffering employees a massive favour.

WONDER WOMAN

Far too important to bother with a label like Ms or Mrs, Wonder Woman has it all: superhuman strength, a golden lasso, an invisible plane, the tiara of a Greek goddess, star-spangled shorts and a formidable peer group that includes a man who can fly faster than the speed of sound, a recluse billionaire crime fighter, a strange fella with an attachment to an emerald lamp and a red suited guy who can run faster than the eye can follow.

And her civilian alter-ego is in some ways even more impressive: the perfect career, the perfect marriage, the perfect children, the perfect house in the country and the perfect villa in the South of France. She is damn good at what she does. In fact she is damn good at everything.

Wonder Woman employs an army of people at home and abroad: an au pair, a nanny, three sets of gardeners, two personal trainers, several cleaners, a washer/ironer, two chefs and a part-time chauffer - whom she collectively refers to as her "infrastructure". She can afford it; Wonder Woman is on the Board and is one of the industry's high flyers. Her employees are in awe of her, even though they find it difficult to relate to her as they don't live in her world. Very few people do.

Wonder Woman is a role model for all women in business, at every level on the corporate ladder. To her, the much-touted "glass ceiling" is utter nonsense; a mythical male construct designed to keep women out of the board room. She is guest speaker at "Woman of the Year" luncheons. She is regularly featured in the Sunday papers. She is the stellar filly in the stable of one of the capital's leading speakers' bureaus, and is constantly in demand. She is the poster girl for 'board diversity'; the living, breathing proof of the benefits of increasing the number of women on boards.

(Which, incidentally, is woefully low. Although the figure has increased by a third in the twelve months leading up to the publication of this book, there are still five men for every woman on the boards of the top 100 firms in the UK. Fifteen of these companies have no female representation whatsoever. Research report after research report has shown that the performance of male-only boards is often sub-optimal, as they are far more susceptible to Group-Think. However, while some progress has been made of late, the age of the male-dominated board is far from over, to the detriment of shareholders, employees and the national economy. Glad to get that off my chest. I shall hop down from my soap box now.)

If you have a Wonder Woman on your board, congratulations. You have a game-changing differentiator in your midst. Through her, you can now find and nurture similarly talented women in your organisation. Through her, you can attract like-minded women from outside your company. She will be able to position your business at the forefront of your industry. Of course, you may have to help her realise that not everyone can live up to her incredible standards; not everyone can successfully juggle career, family, fitness and whirlwind social life to such a superhuman level. But this is one of the few occurrences when Mini-Mees are a good thing.

Two alternative fates await Wonder Woman. The first is that she will wake one day to find her eldest daughter has acquired a very expensive drug habit courtesy of her very expensive public school and her husband is having an affair with the au pair - and one of the chefs. The second scenario is that she continues to shine and is one of those rare and wonderful people who make it to the very top of her chosen career and manage to keep their beautiful family together at the same time.

I am hoping beyond all reason for the latter. The world needs more Wonder Women.

MISSION MAN

Some leaders are *Vision* people. They paint pictures of what the future could look like. They believe in clearly articulating a company's purpose; its reason for being; why it exists. They ask esoteric questions such as "What is this company?" and "What does it stand for?" They believe the future of their business depends upon their ability to motivate their people, and to do that they need to articulate the type of business that all employees can create if they work together.

But others with far more lead in their pencil are *Mission Men*. To Mission Man, a vision is something dreamt up by the Colouring In Department. It is a fairy-tale description of Nirvana; of what the company could look like if all the planets aligned, the doves were let loose to fly free and peace descended upon the Earth.

A Mission on the other hand is proper Men's stuff. It is a Vision that is armed, cocked and ready to fire. Missions have clear objectives, a clear roadmap to achieve them and clear tactics to employ in the heat of battle. A mission-based approach may not be everyone's cup of tea, but you have to admire the fact that its sole purpose is to deliver results.

Mission Man loves Missions. He lives by them, and when he was leading his troops in Afghanistan / Iraq / Bosnia / Iraq / The Falklands / Northern Ireland / Nicaragua / Vietnam / Call of Duty … some of his people even died by them. He knows the importance of 'intel' but he rarely trusts anyone else's analysis of the data put before him. Unfortunately, his past successes have blinded him to the fact that he may not be right this time. In a George Dubya Bush / Anthony Charles Lynton Blair / Alastair John Campbell kind of way, he will select the analysis that best suits his preferred hypothesis.

When Mission Man holds you in his searchlight gaze, you know it. The intensity of his 100% concentration is blinding and can cause even the most confident and experienced executive to begin to question his or her own judgment. It is not that he is a bully; far from it. He is just so assured of his ability to make the right decisions, his ability to command and the action that needs to be taken that his laser-like certainty evaporates all doubts upon contact.

It is only when the searchlight beam turns its attention to another that you are able to blink the stars from your eyes and start to question precisely what just happened. It is

during these contemplative moments of relative darkness that questions are identified and constructive challenges are formed. The only problem is that all too often they will vanish once the beam sweeps around to face you once again.

However, even given the oxymoronic, comic/tragic nature of his Captain Commando approach, Mission Man does what few leaders are able to do: he delivers; and he achieves outstanding results through his people. Mission Man has a great deal to offer and he has a great deal to teach most other executives about the joy of focus and the importance of delivery.

Your challenge is to help him dress these lessons in civilian clothes and make them more palatable to most of us who have never dreamed of joining the Armed Forces. Mission Man also badly needs people around him who can help him hone his thinking and challenge his unflinching certainty. You need to locate these "Missionaries" and deploy them in a way that Mission Man will accept and embrace. Your mission (if you choose to accept it) is to hone Mission Man's talents for the good of the organisation. So, don your Aviators, spit-polish your boots, stiffen your resolve and march into battle. Your company needs you!

MR SUPERFICIAL (AKA ALL-MOUTH-AND-NO-TROUSERS)

Like a water strider skimming across the surface of a pond, Mr Superficial strides across the world of business, never in the slightest danger of getting his feet wet or slipping below the surface.

He is most definitely a Vision Man and the broader the canvas, the bigger the landscape, the better. He is an evangelical exponent of Vision Statements; pithy one-liners designed to summarise the intended future state of the organisation. He has forced his senior management team to spend untold man-days repeatedly word-smithing these greeting card blandishments before sending his managers out to all corners of the company to gain "buy-in" to these beautifully honed phrases from as many people as possible.

He is obsessed with Values and will spend even greater amounts of time and expense hand-crafting six perfectly formed words and chiselling them into the foundation stones of the company. Soon after his reign commences, the walls will become adorned with life-size posters of smiling employees with words such as "Driven", "Fairness", "Integrity" and "Customer-centric" emblazoned above their beaming faces.

He never gets flustered and he rarely gets annoyed. Some say he is like a swan, but if they were to peek below the water-line, they would find that he isn't actually paddling very hard. He is serene because his years of experience have shown him that getting flustered or annoyed or even passionate never did any leader any good whatsoever. Shareholders hate that sort of behaviour and they are, at the end of the day, the ones who pay the bills.

Mr Superficial is an excellent statesman. He is brilliant with the media and always available for comment. He is king of the sound bite and has honed his technique to such a degree that even his lengthy interviews have the feel of someone who knows what they are talking about. Of course, he won't to any great degree, but he certainly knows how to look and sound precisely like someone who does.

Mr Superficial is great with shareholders, too. He listens to them attentively and leaves every single one of them with the sincere belief that their concerns will be addressed with utmost speed.

Mr Superficial is also superb with customers. He listens to their gripes, empathises with their plight, is fascinated with their improvement suggestions and leaves them in no doubt that he believes they are running brilliant businesses in their own right.

The disappointing thing about Mr Superficial is that deep down (actually, no, not so deep down) he just doesn't care. This certainly enables him to remain calm in a crisis, for as long as he can keep his reputation intact, he won't lose one wink of sleep over how well the business is doing. Mr Superficial is most often found in business-to-business organisations. One of the reasons for this is that actual consumers, like employees can spot a pretender miles away.

What to do with Mr Superficial? Well the obvious thing is not to hire him in the first place, but that is easier said than done as he is awfully difficult to spot in an interview. The first step to any rehabilitation programme, is to realise you have a problem. Oh, and by the way, it is your problem, not his. He is a great frontman but you need to plug his gaps and surround him with two types of people – those with in-depth knowledge of the industry, and those who understand operations and are highly capable at delivering. Or just pay him off and start again.

MR ONE-OF-THE-BOYS

Mr One-of-the-Boys is the Peter Pan of the business world.
If Peter Pan can be considered to be a loud, boisterous,
middle-aged man with an endless supply of amusing
anecdotes and fifty-shades-of-blue jokes for every occasion.

He used to play a decent game of rugger twenty years ago,
downing ten pints after each match. Nowadays it's six pints
watching the International at Twickers followed by a steak
béarnaise and a couple of bottles of Bordeaux's finest.
He is the life in an otherwise deathly dull party,
counterbalancing the hair-pulling straightness that is rife
throughout the rest of the organisation. He gives the most
entertaining speeches at management conferences, is
always the last to leave the bar and yet somehow the first to
breakfast, often after nothing more than a quick shower, a
precarious shave and change of suit.

You may be surprised to discover that Mr One-of-the-Boys
looks after Sales.

Life is pretty straightforward for Mr One-of-the-Boys. He
either brings in the numbers and is left alone to indulge
his team in foreign golf trips, motorsports weekends and
lap-dancing clubs; or he doesn't bring in the numbers and

he's fired. And that is just fine with Mr One-of-the-Boys. If only the rest of the Executive Team were judged in such a black-and-white, success-or-failure manner, they may actually get off their backsides and deliver their end of the deal.

Mr One-of-the-Boys loves customers and is convinced that he is the only one who understands their needs or even recognises their importance. In fact, the rest of the human race seems to exist for the sole purpose of frustrating Mr One-of-the-Boys. Marketing has no concept of what actually sells, Finance has never met a customer, Compliance is the Business Prevention Unit, Operations prefer to make no decision than risk making a wrong one, IT lives in a completely different solar system than the rest of the human race and HR is to be avoided at all costs.

Mr One-of-the-Boys can't be bothered with namby-pamby people management rubbish like appraisals or personal development plans. Life is pretty straightforward for his people. They either bring in the numbers and are therefore welcome to join him in the foreign golf trips, motorsports weekends and lap-dancing clubs; or they don't bring in the numbers and they're fired.

In direct contradiction to the conventional rules of magnetism, Mr One-of-the-Boys' unique persona

attracts clones of himself. Very soon, herds of Master One-of-the-Boys will be seen and heard trumpeting around the business.

Mr One-of-the-Boys angrily defends claims that he is sexist. Little Cindy heads up the sales support function and her team of Megan, Trish and Britney do a superb job for the lads. He did employ a female sales rep once but it didn't work out. For some reason, she just didn't seem to fit in. For all his bonhomie, bluff and bluster, Mr One-of-the-Boys has no idea what to do when confronted by Ms Ironballs and becomes completely tongue-tied around Wonder Woman; although Miss Botox is damn good value after a few chardonnays.

There is a four-step process to dealing with Mr One-of-the-Boys. One: assign a minder to stick to him like glue to prevent him from costing the company a small fortune in sexual harassment cases. Two: give him very clear boundaries in terms of what he is allowed to sell and what he is allowed to spend. Three: give him black-and-white targets with no wriggle room. Four: reward him handsomely for exceeding those targets.

Oh and lastly – listen to him. He may actually be the only one who does understand your customers.

MR FIFTEEN MINUTES

Every company has a Mr Fifteen Minutes. In fact, every advertising agency is bound by law to have at least two or three; more often than not they are the men whose names are above the front door. Mr Fifteen Minutes was famous once; extraordinarily so. He had his day in the spotlight; it was a long time ago and it may have only been one day, but he had it.

He was the man behind a world famous beer commercial. He was the driving force behind the stock exchange listing of a large mutual life insurer. His was the successful legal case that enabled a celebrity to escape incarceration. He invented something incredibly useful such as Velcro, Post-it notes or self-adhesive envelopes. He established the product that put the company you work for on the map.

Mr Fifteen Minutes was indeed *The Man* - a decade or two ago - and he has been dining out on it ever since.

It would be cruel to say he was a one-hit-wonder. Sure, he peaked early, but at a height that very few of the rest of us will ever achieve. Many companies revere their Mr Fifteen Minutes. 3M fetes them until retirement, sending them on world-wide tours to explain again and again how they

came upon their invention and how it changed the world. Other companies reward them with large one-off bonuses or swathes of share options in recognition of the shareholder value they have created.

So why do we duck behind the pot plant whenever we see Mr Fifteen Minutes coming our way? Why is our idea of hell to be caught in a broken lift with Mr Fifteen Minutes and the new fawning management trainee who has only heard Mr FM's story five times and still waits wide-eyed on his every word?

Is it something to do with the fact that the world has moved on? Whilst historical success is interesting, future success is obviously the key that drives the world of business. Ask any ex-executive of MG Rover, British Leyland, Compaq, Rank Arena, Lehman Brothers, AIG, ABN Amro, Polaroid, … and they will describe in painful detail how past success means very little if the organisation is incapable of sustaining its historical achievements. Shareholders don't look in the rear vision mirror for long; they are interested in future returns; future growth; future success.

So what to do with Mr Fifteen Minutes? Hmmm. That's a tough one. Sacking a living legend once he has reached his

sell-by date would set a very poor example to the rest of the staff. You can't give an ageing Mr Fifteen Minutes the Mr Teflon treatment for the simple reason that this man has actually achieved something. Celebrating his success is obvious, as is keeping the celebrations going for a duration that is proportional to the size of his achievement. Having him act as a mentor for up and coming talent is also an obvious move, but only for as long as his achievements are relevant and fresh.

The key thing is to make sure the company learns from his success. We often talk about learning from failures, but rarely do we analyse success and learn the lessons from what went right.

In the end, Mr Fifteen Minutes must be allowed to make a gracious exit, so eventually, early retirement with a huge fanfare may be the best solution. Perhaps even a part-time gig in some sort of advisory capacity, where he can continue to relive his past glories with other recently retired executives. But however you decide to engineer his eventual departure, you must treat him well. For the sake of your people and the reputation of the company, Mr Fifteen Minutes needs to go to his grave as a proud advocate of your organisation.

MR GROWTHMAN

During the boom times, when the word "bust" had been officially expunged from our collective lexicon, and when companies dared to invest and grow, the man of the moment was Mr Growthman. Because when a company wants to grow, there is only one person to call.

Mr Growthman is a grown-up version of Mr Excitable. He is a visionary; he's charismatic, he's great with the media and he is someone who leads very much from the front. The rest of the company takes their cues from Mr Growthman. The organisation's culture soon becomes entwined with his personality and his way of doing things.

He sets outrageous goals for the organisation, goals which most of the staff initially believe are utterly fanciful. However, Mr Growthman is not to be underestimated. He is a consummate cat herder; the sheer force of his boundless energy and drive will sweep the entire company along in his wake, enabling his people to achieve outstanding results, to their utter surprise and complete amazement. During the boom times, Mr Growthman is the brightest star in the constellation and he relishes the limelight.

Mr Growthman is an optimist, a pragmatist and a risk taker. He surrounds himself with people who think and act in the same way. Managers who are risk-averse, refuse to take accountability or unwilling to countenance that there may be a better way and that stellar growth is possible to achieve will one day wake up to discover that they have been shunted into a head office job with a great sounding title but no real authority – or they are now working for the competition.

Mr Growthman loathes people who give him problems. He doesn't want to understand why something *can't* be done, he wants to know what *solution* his people have come up with to make sure it *can* be done. He also doesn't want to be bothered with the detail, unless it's sales figures or customer intelligence. He expects his Finance Director to perform miracles with the numbers and for his Compliance/Legal/ (in fact insert any technical department here) Chief to just get on with his job and not get in the way of growth.

Mr Growthman is a 'top line' person. The 'bottom line' is for someone else to concern themselves with and, given enough growth, will take care of itself. If and when profits do start to slow, his answer is either to increase profit margins or to increase top-line sales revenue or both. To Mr Growthman, cost-reduction is an admission of failure. It is the last bastion of the damned. It is for insecure, spineless people who have already thrown in the towel. It is definitely not the Mr Growthman way.

Mr Growthman understands that business inevitably comes in waves, that peaks are inexorably followed by troughs. He is not such a fantasist to believe that he (or anyone else) can banish the economic "boom and bust" cycle, but he does believe he can tame its impact on his business. He also believes that through diversification and exploring multiple channels at once, he can make the troughs as shallow as possible; and through a relentless focus on sales and growth, he can maximise the size of the peaks.

When it comes to corporate politics, his job is to shield his team from it as much as possible. This way they can get on with the job of growing the business. His strategy is very simple – as long as his part of the enterprise is growing, head office will leave him alone and may even support him from time to time.

Of course, the problems start when the cycle inevitably turns and the growth starts to slow; when the troughs deepen faster than he can fill them in and the peaks don't quite hit the highs that he had so confidently predicted.

That is when the politicians come to the fore because in the dog-eat-dog world of big company politics, success not only breeds success, it also breeds resentment. At the first sign that the stellar growth may be coming to an end, the knives will start to appear. After the first major hiccup, the vultures will descend. Never mind that Mr Growthman has quadrupled the size of the business in the last five years, he will soon be yesterday's man and is destined to be shown the exit. Of course it is unfair, but it is the way of the world.

On his way out, there may be time for a quick pause for thought and introspection. Maybe he could have paraded his successes in slightly less of a showboating manner. Perhaps a little humility would have been in order. Maybe he should have spent more time understanding what those sub-prime CDO thingies that the investment guys were piling the customers into were all about. Perhaps his plan of trying to grow the company in every single dimension at the same time was a tad unrealistic … still, little can be gained by dwelling on the past.

It's time to head for the villa in Marbaya, reduce that golf handicap and warm up his impressive network of contacts.

Hopefully Mr Growthman will work out that he can use the cyclical nature of business to his advantage. One of the irrefutable laws of business is that a 'growth' wave will inevitably crest and crash to Earth, to be followed by a period of calm before the sea slowly drags the water out to form the next wave.

Major League Mr Growthman have learnt that the best strategy they can adopt is to jump ship (unfortunately continuing this dubious nautical theme) before the next wave breaks, and take their well-negotiated performance bonus with them to the next becalmed company in need of their services.

And this would be the right thing to do because Mr Growthman is definitely not the man to mop up his own mess.

For that, we need Mr Batten-Down-the-Hatches.

MR BATTEN-DOWN-THE-HATCHES

There comes a time in the life cycle of every business where it needs to retire to its cave and lick its wounds; to cut costs and consolidate. This is the time to call for Mr Batten-Down-the-Hatches.

Not a man blessed with a world-class personality, sense of humour, social grace or any sort of dress sense post 1975, Mr Batten-Down-the-Hatches' job is to slash budgets (sack people), rationalise the company's product offerings (sack people), increase efficiencies (sack people), optimise the customer service departments (reduce service levels and sack people), increase operating efficiencies (streamline processes, introduce more technology and sack people), close down under-performing businesses (sack people), sell off non-core business (reduce debt and indirectly sack people) and increase the company's margins (charge the customers more … and sack people). Inevitably, the first budgets that Mr Batten-Down-the-Hatches will cut will be advertising and staff training, in spite of the fact that these are the very things that the company will need in order to prosper during the next growth phase.

The smart, but incredibly brave, move would be to maintain spending on brand positioning, advertising and learning

& development during the down turn. Imagine a company that believed in its future enough to make sure that, once the economic cycle started to swing upwards, it had worked during the lean times to retain its customers, hold on to its best people and ensure they had developed the skills that were needed to grow the company. The next Mr Growthman will just have to reintroduce these indulgent luxuries when he returns a few years hence.

For this is Mr Batten-Down-the-Hatches' blind spot. He isn't a long term thinker – he's a short term numbers man. He doesn't recognise that letting people go only to hire them back again in the not-too-distant future is an outrageously expensive exercise. He doesn't see that investing in developing talent is much cheaper than hiring more senior people – and that the former approach also engenders loyalty and greater productivity. Mr Batten-Down-the-Hatches doesn't make a lot of friends but, as he repeatedly says to anyone who is within earshot, that's not why he was hired.

It's not that Mr Batten-Down-the-Hatches doesn't believe in growth. Of course he does. That would be like not believing in sunshine! He just doesn't believe in profligacy. To him,

growth can only be obtained from a solid financial footing; a sensible cost base with as little debt as possible. A sound argument. The only problem is that to achieve this financial heaven, our anti-hero inevitably had to cut far deeper than he expected, thus hampering the company's ability to bounce back in the future.

Once the company is back on its feet and the legal, audit and finance departments are happily in control once again, it will inevitably be time to think of growing the company once more.

This should be the exit cue for Mr Batten-Down-the-Hatches, but more often than not he will tend to outstay his welcome. Mr Batten-Down-the-Hatches has no idea how to grow the company; that's Mr Growthman's job. If you're not very careful, Mr Batten-Down-the-Hatches may transmogrify into good old Mr Improbable, fooling himself that he can be Mr Growthman after all. He can't. Don't let him. Thank him for the job he's done, pay him off and move him onto the next basket case organisation that needs 'turning around'.

Otherwise, he will stuff things up even worse than the next Mr Growthman eventually will.

MR PERFECT

And finally we come to Mr Perfect. He is simply marvellous.

He has the gravitas of Mr Intimidator but combines this with an approachable humility. He has the drive of Mr Excitable and the maturity of vision and media instincts of Mr Growthman. He has the keenness of eye of Mr Velcro Hands but gives the credit to those who deserve it. He has the resilience of Mr Teflon but takes the rap for anything that goes wrong. He has the people management and development skills of Mrs I-Love-Work-It-Gets-Me-Away-From-The-Kids but somehow seems to have the time to devote hours to each of his direct reports. He has the financial acumen of Mr Batten-Down-the-Hatches which he uses to ensure that the growth is sustainable and that his operations department is capable of supporting future growth.

Mr Perfect is both a Vision Man and a Mission Man, able to combine strategic clarity with a relentless drive for delivery. He takes accountability, makes decisions and shares the spoils. Customers love him, employees love him and shareholders simply adore him.

Unfortunately, he doesn't exist.

43

SO WHAT DOES A GOOD LEADER LOOK LIKE?

"Leadership: it's the art of getting someone else to do something you want done because he wants to do it."
(Dwight D Eisenhower)

To be embarrassingly trite for a moment, a leader is simply someone whom people wish to follow. A *good* leader, however, also knows - and cares - where he or she is taking them.

But before I begin my description of what a good leader looks like, let me be completely clear: There is no absolute right or wrong way to lead and even good leaders are human and will have their bad days.

However, a good leader must be able to do a few straightforward things …

They must possess the ability to paint the big picture for their people, shareholders and customers. They give their people an aspiration to aim for.

They must be able to set a vision of the future that is both credible and captures their employee's imaginations. They must also be capable of driving, inspiring, encouraging and enabling people to achieve that vision.

Good leaders care passionately about their company, their customers, their people and the future they are aiming to achieve. They are not just in it for the money or the status.

A good leader appreciates that leadership is a privilege, not a birth right. A good leader appreciates that everyone in the organisation has placed their trust in them, and is fully aware of the responsibility that goes hand-in-hand with this.

A good leader realises that the company's customers are the number one reason that it exists. Employees come a very, very close second and shareholders third, Never, ever should this list be in any other order.

A good leader knows that if you deliver products and services that customers crave, and treat your people with the respect they deserve whilst empowering them to deliver in the way they believe is best for the customer, the results will come and the shareholders will be richly rewarded. Leaders who start with the shareholder in mind will inevitably be unable to think beyond next month's figures and will be setting themselves up for a major clash with customers and staff – to the detriment of everyone, especially the shareholders they were trying so desperately to please in the first place.

A good leader understands and empathises with their customers. They know their needs and, of even higher importance, their wants and they focus their company on meeting these expectations. A good leader puts the customer at the heart of the organisation and his people strive to ensure that every customer experience enhances the reputation of the company.

A good leader invites their people to find innovative solutions to problems and seek out new opportunities. They understand and empathise with their people, whilst simultaneously driving them to deliver outrageous results. Good leaders command and receive a respect that is based on admiration rather than fear.

Good leaders understand that employees need to be emotionally committed to the organisation. Not only must every employee know what they personally need to do to deliver the strategy, but they must also be motivated to do so. While *rational* motivation is important (i.e. the logical reason for why each objective needs to be achieved), *emotional* motivation is the secret to success (i.e. when each employee has identified the personal benefit to them associated with delivery of the objective).

Good leaders give their people enough freedom to take decisions and make mistakes without fearing the consequences.

Good leaders aren't afraid to make decisions themselves, even when they don't have all the information to hand and they aren't afraid to change them when the evidence points in a different direction. Good leaders also don't mind making mistakes, because they learn from them. And good leaders aren't afraid to make tough, even unpopular decisions.

Good leaders are not afraid to show their weaknesses. In fact, they hire people to compensate for them. Good leaders hire people who are better than they are and have the confidence to get out of their way.

Good leaders invest in developing their people, understanding that they are the only genuine source of long-term competitive advantage. Good leaders develop several people as their potential successors, because even those who don't get promoted will move on to bigger and better things outside of the organisation – and they will be motivated to deliver outstanding results in the meantime.

A good leader is obsessed with the delivery of tangible business outcomes, not obsessing over details of the process that should have been followed or whether a project's action items have been completed. Effort is admirable but ultimately irrelevant. A good leader knows that delivery and results are paramount.

"I start with the premise that the function of leadership is to produce more leaders, not more followers." (Ralph Nader)

Great leaders embrace stewardship, working to leave the organisation in a better state than they inherited from the leaders before them.

Great leaders are confident enough in their own abilities and secure enough in their own sense of self-worth to enable other people to develop their own leadership skills.

Great leaders also do one other thing, exceptionally well. We all have an in-built insincerity sensor; we find it very easy to tell when someone is trying to pretend to be someone they're not. So above all, great leaders are not afraid to be themselves.

CREATING EXTRAORDINARY LEADERSHIP TEAMS

While it is vitally important that your organisation's leaders are doing the best job possible, most of the results in today's collegiate, meritocratic, open-plan business world is managed and performed by teams. So I couldn't let the book finish without a quick chat about how to make sure you get the most out of that most important of crews; your organisation's leadership team.

Many employees look at their company's leadership team with a mixture of awe and bemusement; awe at the confidence, wealth and sense of self-worth of the diners at the corporation's top table; and bemusement as to how they got there and the lengths to which some of them will go to keep their place as long as possible.

Why is it that in many organisations, the closer you get to the board room, the closer the behaviour is likely to resemble that of the kindergarten? Egos, personal agendas, bullying behaviour, inability to share … can be seen magnified around many a board table across the globe.

Just two of many examples I have come across include:

1. Differences of opinion almost came to blows during a board meeting of one of the world's largest banks as the Group Marketing Director dared to disagree with the pronouncements forthcoming from the all-conquering head of the Investment Banking arm.
2. The board of one of the leading global pharmaceutical companies has been described by an insider as "a pack of Alpha males trying to score points off one another."

And family businesses can often be worse, as childhood pecking orders and ancient squabbles come to the fore during times of stress, and family members promoted over more competent employees.

Of course, the vast majority of leadership teams don't behave like this (or at least not all the time!), so what is it that makes these leadership teams effective? Or better still, *what makes a leadership team extraordinary?*

Having been a member of several leadership teams and seen countless dozens more in action across a variety of different industries over the last three decades, I have come to the conclusion that in order to be extraordinary, leadership teams need to maximise their effectiveness, simultaneously, across three dimensions:

1. Individual Effectiveness
2. Team Effectiveness
3. Effectiveness as a Leader

Extraordinary leadership teams need all three dimensions – in equal balance.

If you genuinely want your leadership team to be extraordinary, you cannot skimp on any one of these, and you cannot be overweight in one of them in the hope that this will make up for a deficiency in another.

Extraordinary leadership teams are made up of confident, effective leaders who respect and trust one another. They must respect one another's ability to deliver (individual effectiveness), ability to lead their respective departments (effectiveness as a leader) and ability to be a highly effective team member (team effectiveness).

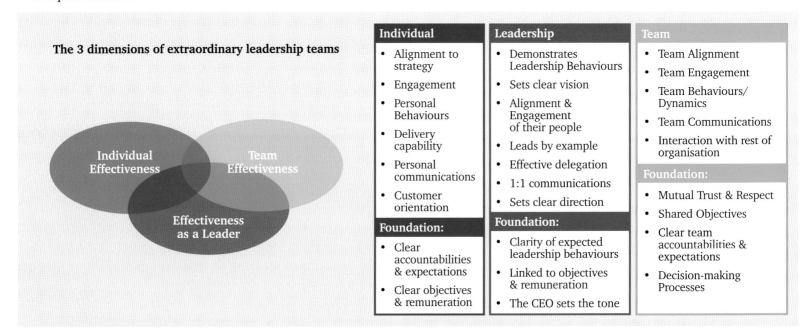

The 3 dimensions of extraordinary leadership teams

Individual Effectiveness

Team Effectiveness

Effectiveness as a Leader

Individual
- Alignment to strategy
- Engagement
- Personal Behaviours
- Delivery capability
- Personal communications
- Customer orientation

Foundation:
- Clear accountabilities & expectations
- Clear objectives & remuneration

Leadership
- Demonstrates Leadership Behaviours
- Sets clear vision
- Alignment & Engagement of their people
- Leads by example
- Effective delegation
- 1:1 communications
- Sets clear direction

Foundation:
- Clarity of expected leadership behaviours
- Linked to objectives & remuneration
- The CEO sets the tone

Team
- Team Alignment
- Team Engagement
- Team Behaviours/ Dynamics
- Team Communications
- Interaction with rest of organisation

Foundation:
- Mutual Trust & Respect
- Shared Objectives
- Clear team accountabilities & expectations
- Decision-making Processes

The secret ingredients to building extraordinary leadership teams:

Clarity. Clarity is essential; if the leadership team isn't genuinely clear about where the organisation is going, why, what needs to be done and who is accountable for delivering what … the rest of the organisation has no chance. The implications of the strategy need to be fully understood and there needs to be utter clarity regarding the expectations and accountabilities of each individual executive as well as the leadership team as a whole.

Alignment. A successful team needs to be aligned around this clear strategy. They need to ensure that everything they are doing both individually and collectively is working towards achieving the corporate goals.

Engagement. The team must be involved in defining the above, not just implementing it. Only when people have had a hand in the design will they be fully engaged in, and committed to, delivering the outcomes.

Clearly defined rules of engagement. A successful team defines what good looks like in terms of team dynamics. How team members behave; how the team works is just as important as what it needs to deliver. To be a truly extraordinary team, each team member needs to give the others permission to tell them when they are not displaying the agreed behaviours.

Shared objectives. A team can be genuinely effective only if they are all striving to achieve the same things. If every Executive is focused on achieving their own individual objectives rather than the organisation's goals, they will never become a high performing team.

Respect. Each team member needs to develop respect for the skills and experience and abilities that each of their colleagues brings to the table. Understanding one another's strengths and weaknesses is important as a person's key strength is often also their key weakness. But let's keep some sense of perspective; this is a business, not a marriage.

A team of extraordinary leaders. Each member of the leadership team must be a leader in their own right. The team needs to define the leadership behaviours they are going to display, how they are going to live up to these expectations, the ramifications if they don't and how they are going to continually develop their leadership skills.

No magic pill. Whilst a great deal can be achieved through specific interventions, this is a journey. Extraordinary teams evolve, they are not created overnight.

Campbell

campbell@campbellmacpherson.co.uk
www.campbellmacpherson.co.uk

THE BLATANT ADVERTISING BIT AT THE END

If you would like the leaders in your organisation to be a little more like Mr Perfect and a whole lot less like Mr Teflon …
If you would like your leadership team to be extraordinary …
Or even if you have spotted a leader we have missed …

Get in contact!

Campbell Macpherson & Associates is a small but perfectly formed band of business change experts.
We help CEOs, HR Directors, leadership teams and boards improve the way their organisations work.

Common issues:

The business not fulfilling its potential	Poor understanding of customers
Poor understanding of the strategy	Key accountabilities unclear
Leadership team effectiveness	Key issues remain unresolved
Culture holding the business back	Board Effectiveness Review due

Our solutions:

Alignment & Engagement	Customer Experience Review	Strategy Alignment Methodology
Strategy Articulation & Review	Organisation Design	Org Design Methodology
Extraordinary Leadership Teams	Hunting for Elephants	Alignment & Culture Surveys
Culture Development	Board Effectiveness Review	Org Effectiveness Survey

60 Lombard Street
London EC3V 9EA

Campbell Macpherson & Associates
Improving the way organisations work

www.campbellmacpherson.co.uk
+44 (0)20 3427 3959